GRIMSL
AND
CLEETHORPES
TROLLEYBUSES

Colin Barker
Series editor Robert J Harley

MP Middleton Press

Cover Picture: This view, taken at Cleethorpes Bathing Pool in August 1955, depicts a vehicle from each municipality in their respective liveries with Grimsby AEC 9 in the foreground. Its dark crimson lake livery looks a little on the purple side; a Cleethorpes vehicle brings up the rear. Although this view has been used in an earlier publication, quality coloured photographs including vehicles from both operators have been difficult to find hence its use here. (B Jenkins)

Builders initials
AEC Associated Equipment Company
BUT British United Traction

Published September 2006

ISBN 1 904474 86 1

© *Middleton Press, 2006*

Design Deborah Esher

Published by
> *Middleton Press*
> *Easebourne Lane*
> *Midhurst, West Sussex*
> *GU29 9AZ*

Tel: 01730 813169
Fax: 01730 812601
Email: info@middletonpress.co.uk
www.middletonpress.co.uk

Printed & bound by Biddles Ltd, Kings Lynn

CONTENTS

INTRODUCTION AND ACKNOWLEDGMENTS

The concept of two undertakings operating trolleybuses over the same overhead wiring has always been of interest ever since my first sighting of a blue and cream Notts & Derby Traction vehicle amongst Nottingham's green and cream trolleybuses during a childhood visit in the early 1940s. Further travels in later years provided sightings of the Manchester/Ashton, St Helens/South Lancashire and Walsall/Wolverhampton joint workings. Compiling this volume on the small Grimsby and Cleethorpes' systems has therefore been particularly enjoyable, although I never saw them in operation.

This book is not intended to be a definitive history of the systems but more a pictorial journey which should jog the memories of older generations, whilst illustrating to others a form of public transport they will only ever see in operation when they travel abroad. The views follow the main joint Route 11 between Grimsby Old Market Place through to the Bathing Pool in Cleethorpes, plus the opening Grimsby Route 10 from Riby Square to Weelsby Road.

In preparing my two earlier volumes for this series I have had the advantage of focusing on my home town of Derby and my adopted town of Ipswich, the latter having a thriving transport museum with comprehensive local archive material. Being unfamiliar with Grimsby and Cleethorpes it has been necessary to research the local geography and be aware of the changes, particularly in Grimsby, that have occurred since the closure of the system. The help of local enthusiast Alan Tye has been invaluable. He has given much of his time to answering my many questions and points of detail, and I am indebted to him. Stan Letts also helped with the identification of the Walsall views and Ken Pudsey, a member of The Transport Ticket Society, provided the sample tickets. Alan Tye, Richard Brooks and Malcolm Hall made valuable suggestions on reading through the first draft. Thanks also to Terry Russell for the line drawing of the vehicles and to Godfrey Croughton for tickets.

The photographs have been provided from many sources, the majority taken by individual enthusiasts who have been generous in agreeing to their use; where the source is known due accreditation has been given. However, it has been impossible to trace the origin of some views and I hope the photographers/copyright holders will understand their views have been chosen to enhance this publication for a wider audience. Other sources of material include the Garrett Long Shop Museum, Ipswich Transport Museum, Beaulieu Motor Museum and the articles of Malcolm Cadey which-- were published in the Grimsby Evening Telegraph. Thanks also go to John Gillham for agreeing to the use of his excellent overhead wiring map and for the continued support and assistance of my wife Maureen.

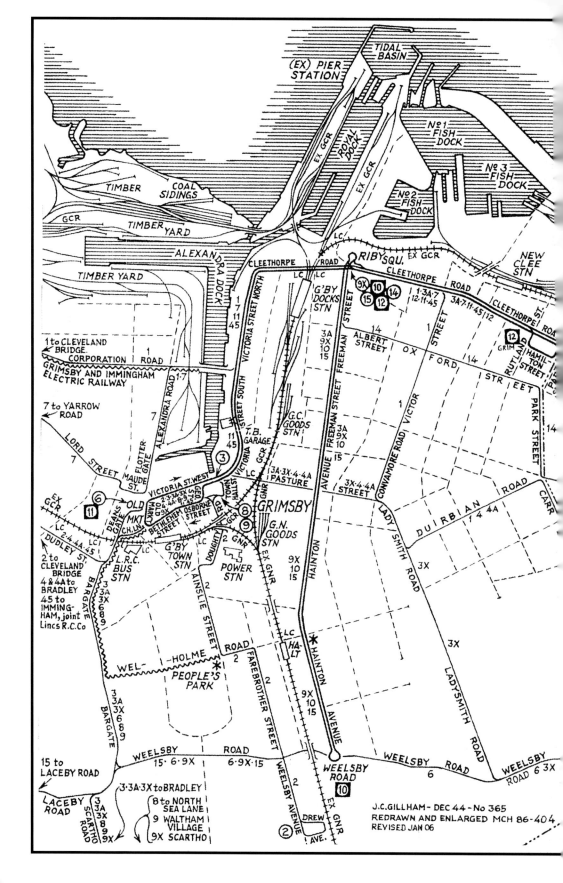

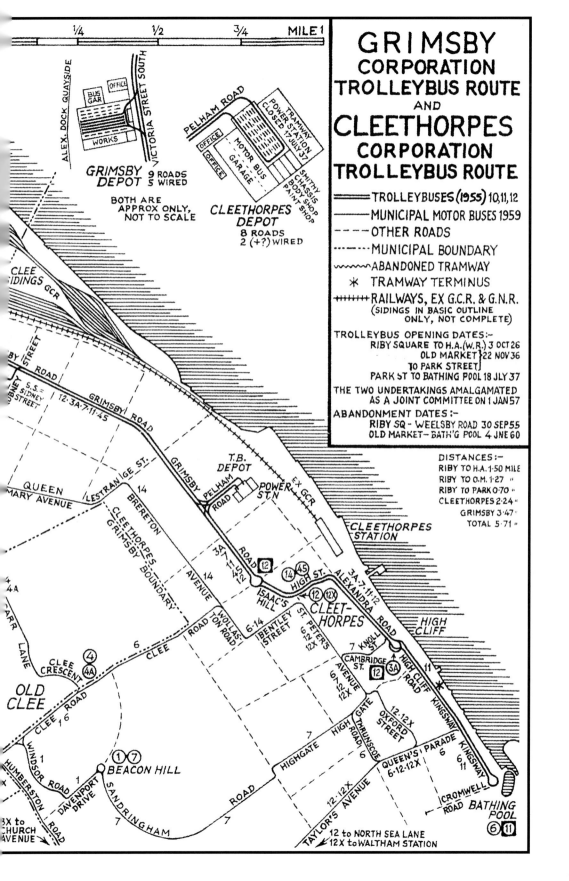

GRIMSBY CORPORATION TROLLEYBUS ROUTE

AND

CLEETHORPES CORPORATION TROLLEYBUS ROUTE

——— TROLLEYBUSES (1955) 10,11,12
——— MUNICIPAL MOTOR BUSES 1959
- - - - OTHER ROADS
······· MUNICIPAL BOUNDARY
〰〰〰 ABANDONED TRAMWAY
   ✳ TRAMWAY TERMINUS
++++++ RAILWAYS, EX G.C.R. & G.N.R.
(SIDINGS IN BASIC OUTLINE
ONLY, NOT COMPLETE)

TROLLEYBUS OPENING DATES:—
RIBY SQUARE TO H.A.(W.R.) 3 OCT 26
OLD MARKET } 22 NOV 36
TO PARK STREET }
PARK ST TO BATHING POOL 18 JLY 37

THE TWO UNDERTAKINGS AMALGAMATED
AS A JOINT COMMITTEE ON 1 JAN 57

ABANDONMENT DATES:—
RIBY SQ - WEELSBY ROAD 30 SEP 55
OLD MARKET - BATH'G POOL 4 JNE 60

DISTANCES:—
RIBY TO H.A. 1·50 MILE
RIBY TO O.M. 1·27 "
RIBY TO PARK 0·70 "
CLEETHORPES 2·24 "
GRIMSBY 3·47 "
TOTAL 5·71 "

GRIMSBY DEPOT 9 ROADS 5 WIRED

BOTH ARE APPROX ONLY, NOT TO SCALE

CLEETHORPES DEPOT 8 ROADS 2 (+?) WIRED

TRAMWAY POWER STATION CLOSED 17 JULY 37

SMITHY
CHASSIS
BODY SHOP
PAINT SHOP

MOTOR BUS GARAGE

OFFICE
OFFICE

PELHAM ROAD

ALEX. DOCK QUAYSIDE

BUS GAR
OFFICE
WORKS

VICTORIA STREET SOUTH

CLEE SIDINGS GCR

BY STREET
UBNEY ROAD
S.S. SIDNEY STREET
12·3A·7·11·45

GRIMSBY ROAD

QUEEN MARY AVENUE
LESTRANGE ST.
BRERETON
CLEETHORPES-GRIMSBY BOUNDARY
AVENUE

14
14

T.B. DEPOT
PELHAM ROAD
POWER STN

EX GCR

CLEETHORPES STATION

3A·7·11·12
ALEXANDRA ROAD

HIGH CLIFF

HIGH CLIFF ROAD

KINGSWAY

3A·14·12
12
14 45
HIGH ST.

ISAAC'S HILL
BENTLEY STREET
ST. PETER'S
6·12·12X

CLEET-HORPES

12 12X

6·14
WOLLASTON ROAD
ROAD

CARR LANE
CLEE CRESCENT
4
4A

OLD CLEE

CLEE ROAD
6

7 KNOLL ST.
CAMBRIDGE ST.
12
3A

11

KINGSWAY

CLEE ROAD
1·6

HIGHGATE
AVENUE
HIGH GATE ROAD
THRUNSCOE ROAD

OXFORD STREET

12·12X
QUEEN'S PARADE
6·12·12X
6
11

1 7
BEACON HILL
1

WINDSOR ROAD
DAVENPORT DRIVE
SANDRINGHAM ROAD

ROAD
7

TAYLOR'S AVENUE

12·12X

CROMWELL ROAD
BATHING POOL
6 11

3X to CHURCH AVENUE

12 to NORTH SEA LANE
12X to WALTHAM STATION

1/4   1/2   3/4   MILE 1

GEOGRAPHICAL AND HISTORICAL SETTING

Grimsby and Cleethorpes are situated on the north east coast of Lincolnshire overlooking the River Humber estuary and are 2.75 miles (4km) apart.

Grimsby was founded by the Danes in the 9th century AD and showed a population of over 200 by the time of the Doomsday Book (1086). Grimsby developed into a port around a river called The Haven which provided the protection for shipping it suggests and it is the fifth oldest Borough having been granted a Charter in 1201. In the 15th century The Haven began to silt up, which reduced activity at the port, leading to a long period of decline for the town.

In 1801 the Grimsby Haven Company opened a dock in the town and a new company was formed in 1845 to build an additional dock in anticipation of the arrival of the railway and in 1848 the Manchester, Sheffield and Lincolnshire Railway (MS&LR) arrived and took control. During this period the population had increased to 8860 by 1851.

Between 1850 and 1879 various new docks were opened to support the growing fishing industry and commercial activities with their ready markets in the urban areas served by the railway. In 1852 the town's famous Dock Tower was completed. In 1889 the town boundary was extended and County Borough status granted in 1891; both of these events were against the background of a continued growth in population.

By the 1920's Grimsby had become one of the largest and most prosperous fishing ports in the world with today's activities only being a shadow of this high point. In 1934 the London North Eastern Railway (LNER) opened a further fish dock.

Cleethorpes grew out of the village of Clee, which was a popular bathing spot as early as the 1830's, and in April 1863 the MS&LR opened a single line railway extension from Grimsby Dock to Cleethorpes terminating in a station adjacent to the beach. Between 1851 and 1871 the population increased to 1768 and the rail line from Grimsby was doubled in 1874.

In 1894 the Cleethorpes-with-Thrunscoe Urban District Council was formed and by 1901 the population had grown to 12578. Boundary extensions took place in 1922/1927 and Cleethorpes Urban District Council (having been created in 1915) was incorporated as a Municipal Borough in September 1936.

In 1996 the two boroughs were combined to form the new county of North East Lincolnshire.

The operating area of both systems was generally flat, with the exception being Isaacs Hill in Cleethorpes that led to the High Street and onwards to Alexandra Road, plus the more gradual incline of High Cliff Road.

HISTORICAL BACKGROUND
TO PUBLIC TRANSPORT

The history of the two trolleybus systems has a common heritage from the original Great Grimsby Street Tramways Company that ran between the two towns.

Three miles (4.4km) of standard gauge were authorised and construction began in 1880, whilst the new company/parent operated horse buses between the two towns.

In 1898 the company notified the two authorities that it was to apply for an Act to electrify the system with a postponement of the right to purchase for 21 years.

The first electric tram left Pelham Road Depot on 7th December 1901 and the service from Riby Square along Freeman Street followed with an extension to Welholme Road. The service to Peoples Park beyond The Wheatsheaf opened on 15th February 1902.

In July 1906 a short extension was opened along High Cliff Road, Cleethorpes to the beginning of Kingsway and in 1909 the parent company, Provincial, introduced its first motorbus.

From 1920 there was growing pressure on Grimsby Corporation to operate its own trams in the borough and it proceeded to promote a Bill to this end. In 1921 the Bill received Royal Assent; Grimsby Corporation Tramways began on 6th April 1925.

By 1925 the tram track in Freeman Street was in poor condition with single track and passing loops and in September 1925 it was decided to convert the route to trolleybuses with an extension to the junction with Weelsby Road. Access to the depot from Riby Square was by use of a trailing skate and the service opened to the paying public on 3rd October 1926 with five Garrett single deckers. Whilst tram track was being removed, time headways increased and it is reported a trolleybus was hired from Ipswich until the purchase of two more Garrett single deckers that arrived in March 1927.

In 1927 Grimsby obtained an Act which absorbed some surrounding districts, provided for the use of motorbuses within the new boundaries and allowed for the substitution of trams by trolleybuses or motorbuses plus route extensions. Cleethorpes insisted the tram track between Riby Square and Park Street be retained for a period of six years to cater for dock and football traffic.

In June 1928 the trams beyond Old Market Place along Bargate were replaced by a new motorbus service. Also in the same year Cleethorpes UDC obtained an Act to operate the tramway in their area and introduce trolleybuses. They were advised they would have to purchase the generating equipment with the tramway, the company already having refused an offer of £20,000 for the tramway alone. Not wishing to be exposed to arbitration, the Council did not take up the option to purchase and also declined a 1932 offer by the company to convert to trolleybuses, if given a new operating agreement.

In June 1935 Grimsby Council decided to replace trams between Old Market Place and Park Street with trolleybuses, although the track was to be left for tram operated dock and football specials as far as Riby Square. A Provisional Order was obtained and ten AEC six wheeled trolleybuses ordered, which allowed the service to commence on 22nd November 1936. Trams continued between Riby Square and Cleethorpes resulting in an overlapping operation between Riby Square and Park Street until 31st March 1937. The few remaining Grimsby trams for the above were housed at Pelham Road, Cleethorpes to allow removal of track between Old Market Place and Riby Square.

In September 1935 the company indicated it was willing to sell the remaining part of its operation to Cleethorpes UDC on the basis of a Ministry of Transport valuation. The Council agreed and obtained the necessary Provisional Order to run trams and convert to trolleybuses with an extension of the latter along Kingsway to the Bathing Pool. So on 15th July 1936 Cleethorpes UDC began its short life as an operator of public transport, since on 23rd September 1936 it was granted Borough status and vehicles then carried the wording "Cleethorpes Corporation Transport". The Great Grimsby Street Tramways Company was wound up on 7th December 1936. Grimsby withdrew its last tram on 31st March 1937 with the remaining Cleethorpes trams continuing to operate as far as Park Street pending the conversion to trolleybuses.

The Cleethorpes trolleybus system opened on 18th July 1937, using ten AEC four wheeled vehicles bodied by Park Royal. The through joint service between the two towns was reinstated. Three similar vehicles were added to the fleet in 1938. Turning facilities from the Grimsby direction were provided at Park Street and High Cliff and from the Cleethorpes direction via a separate loop at Park Street and at Riby Square. A turning circle from the Grimsby direction was provided at the bottom of Isaacs Hill in 1957. All these short workings usually carried Route 12 up to 1957.

Grimsby received a further nine double deck Karrier trolleybuses in 1944 (utility design) and 1947, replacing the original single deck Garretts and Cleethorpes acquired four BUTs and two Crossleys in 1950/51. Four of the original fleet had been sold to Nottingham in 1940. There is a further unsubstantiated report that an Ipswich trolleybus was hired by Grimsby during the 1939-45 war. The combined fleets had a maximum complement of 30 for a short period in 1939 and 29 in the early 1950's.

In October 1955 the Grimsby Freeman Street/Weelsby Road route was converted to motorbus operation and on 1st January 1957 the two undertakings were merged being controlled by a Joint Grimsby-Cleethorpes Transport Committee. The joint fleet comprised 13 Grimsby and 9 operational Cleethorpes trolleybuses, with the latter having 100 added to their fleet numbers. A new livery of mid-blue and cream was used with vehicles displaying both towns' crests.

Pelham Road Depot was closed operationally in March 1957 and trolleybus operations ended on 4th June 1960. Five of Grimsby's Karriers were purchased by Bradford for subsequent rebodying and reuse. This did not come to pass as the new bodies were allocated to ex-Mexborough and Swinton chassis and the Grimsby vehicles used for spares before scrapping. The Cleethorpes BUTs and Crossleys were sold on to Walsall Corporation for further service.

(lower left) Cleethorpes residents and ratepayers discount ticket.
1937. Printed by Bell Punch Co.

(lower right) Cleethorpes cross boundary ticket.
Early 1940s. Printed by Harland.

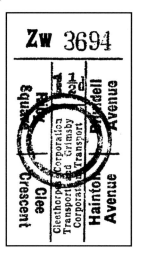

Fares.

TRAMWAYS.				Ordinary Fare	Children over 3 years and under 12 years of of age.
Old Market Place and Riby Square	..	..	..	1d.	
Corporation Road and Humber Street	..	..	..	1d.	½d.
Riby Square and Park Street	..	..	..	1d.	
Old Market Place and Park Street	..	..	..	1½d.	1d.
TROLLEY VEHICLES.					
Riby Square and Welholme Road	..	..	..	1d.	½d.
Hainton Square and Weelsby Road	..	..	..	1d.	
Riby Square and Weelsby Road	..	..	..	1½d.	1d.

Fare chart 1928

(left) Cleethorpes early 1940s.
Printed by Harland

(right) Grimsby workman ticket 1950.
Printed by Bell Punch Co.

(lower left) Grimsby Cross Boundry. 1950.
Printed by Bell Punch Co.

(lower centre) Grimsby Workman return double
journey. 1946. Printed by Bell Punch Co.

(lower right) Joint Committee ticket. 1957.
Printed by Bell Punch Co.

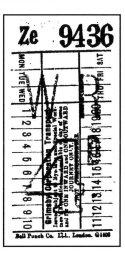

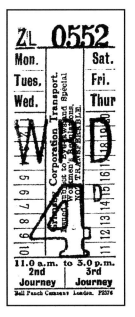

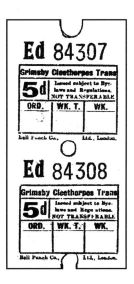

TRAMS TO TROLLEYBUSES

1. Grimsby AEC 18, which in registration sequence should have carried the unused 13 fleet number, was from the batch of vehicles that replaced the Grimsby trams on the main inter-town route as far as Park Street with one of the latter just in view on the left. An indication of the changeover is illustrated by the nearside windscreen reflection of both tram and trolleybus overhead whilst passengers wait to board via the central entrance. (AEI)

2. This view is taken at the Park Street boundary between the two towns looking along Grimsby Road towards Cleethorpes. Tram 39, an ex-Great Grimsby Street Tramways vehicle, owned by Cleethorpes since 15th July 1936, gets ready to make the return trip to Kingsway under newly erected trolleybus overhead. Grimsby were running trolleybuses to Park Street from November 1936. The days of trams along Grimsby Road are numbered to be replaced by the joint through trolleybus service between Old Market Place and the Bathing Pool, when Cleethorpes first trolleybuses enter service in July 1937. Cleethorpes only operated trams for twelve months after purchasing their operation from the private company. The first part of this period was as an Urban District Council and the remainder as a Borough Council. (A D Packer)

GRIMSBY -
GEORGE, OSBORNE & BETHLEHEM STREETS

3.   We start this photographic journey at the beginning of the single loop overhead that led into Grimsby Old Market Place. Grimsby Karrier W 22, in joint ownership livery of mid-blue and cream, has just left the double overhead of Victoria Street West in the left background and entered George Street which in turn leads into Osborne Street, South St Mary's Gate and Bethlehem Street. The hoarding advertisements all feature chocolate products, whilst the learner driver improves driving skills behind the wheel of a three-wheeled Reliant Regal. The Old Kings Head pub is in the background of this May 1957 view. (J Copland / C Routh)

→ 4. Blue and grey liveried Cleethorpes BUT 59 seems to be holding the attention of the little girl by the pram as it leaves the George Street stop and moves into Osborne Street on the last leg of the journey from its home town in May 1952. (A D Packer)

→ 5. Cleethorpes BUT 62, now 162 in joint ownership, has left George Street and continues along the single loop in Osborne Street towards South St Mary's Gate and Bethlehem Street on its way to the Old Market Place in June 1960. An Austin A40 Somerset approaches the pedestrian crossing and the rear of a Wolseley 4/44 car can be seen in the foreground.   (A B Cross)

6.   Cleethorpes Crossley 64 (now 164) makes its way along Bethlehem Street and is about to enter the Old Market Place. The view was taken on the last day of trolleybus operation on 4th June 1960 and depicts Eason's Travel Agency on the corner of the Market Place plus the Yarborough Hotel on the extreme right. (J Copland/C Routh)

GRIMSBY'S NEW TROLLEY CARS

GREAT IMPROVEMENT ON THE TRAMS

SWIFT AND NOISELESS PROGRESS

THE introduction yesterday of trackless trolley cars to replace trams, between the Old Market and Park-street, marks another stage in the development of Grimsby's transport facilities.

The new cars had full complements to-day, passengers being quick to make favourable comparisons between their swift and noiseless progress and the jar and rattle of the old tramcars.

They have, from the point of view of hurried business people one disadvantage. The automatically closing doors make it impossible for passengers to board or alight between stages, as they made a habit of doing when the old tramcars slowed down or stopped in traffic blocks.

HORSE TRAMS

Many of the older residents who patronised the trolley cars can remember the horse trams which plied between Grimsby and Cleethorpes. In those days they went no further than the bottom of Isaac's Hill, as its slope was too steep for a horse-drawn vehicle. When, later, the level of the hill was reduced to enable the trams to go through into Cleethorpes, a spare horse was kept at the bottom of Isaac's Hill and hitched on to help in the pull up.

Electric cars were first introduced on December 7, 1901, and the tramcars were taken over by the Corporation on April 6, 1925.

23 November 1936

GRIMSBY -
OLD MARKET PLACE

7.   Now moving round the Old Market Place we start on the south east side with Grimsby Karrier W 23 in joint ownership, having arrived from Bethlehem Street on the left. In the background is the four-storey Yarborough Hotel with the shops of Alfred Harvey and confectioners Charles Clow prominent on the right. (S Lockwood collection)

◄———— 8. Almost in the same position in August 1958, Cleethorpes AEC 54 (now 154) is still in its municipal blue and grey livery notwithstanding joint ownership. The old fleet number of 54 on the front panel has been painted over and the new number introduced by adding 100 using smaller Grimsby style numerals; this may be because this vehicle was transferred to the Grimsby garage at the time of amalgamation. Alfred Harvey's shop is again in view with the signboard indicating the proprietors were A A Harvey and J Hyde. (A B Cross)

◄———— 9. With the Harvey premises as background Cleethorpes AEC 52 in blue and grey livery, and advertising a local fishmonger, waits to move round the Old Market Place in August 1952. The larger fleet number characters used by Cleethorpes can be seen; note the front inspection panel has an eleven louvre ventilation pattern. The similar vehicle from the same batch seen in Picture 13 has a twenty-two pattern with smaller louvres. (R Marshall)

10. Vehicles from both municipalities are depicted in this view with the dark crimson lake and cream liveried Grimsby Karrier W 19 in the foreground on a short working to the borough boundary at Park Street and Cleethorpes BUT 60 to the rear. The roof line plaque on the building in the foreground indicates a build date of 1929; from photographic evidence the shop below frequently changed hands. (C Carter)

1.   This wartime scene is full of atmosphere with a Cleethorpes AEC, complete with blackout white edging and masked headlights, moving empty from the south east side of the Old Market Place around the sharp bend to the north west. In the foreground is an ARP van (Air Raid Precautions) and beyond the busy market stalls a target thermometer for a campaign called "Salute the Soldier" to raise money for the war effort. Buildings of note are the imposing Corn Exchange beyond the market, Turner's Drapery Store on the left and the White Hart public house on the right. (Courtesy of Grimsby Evening Telegraph)

12.   Grimsby wartime utility Karrier W 2 ⟶   13. Cleethorpes pre-war AEC begins the turn from the south east side on a 57 completes the same manoeuvre ready to short working to the borough boundary at Park depart on the through route to Cleethorpes Street with the Corn Exchange and market in Bathing Pool. A full view of the imposing Corn the background. These vehicles were known Exchange tower can be seen; the foundation as "doodlebugs" by the crews because of their stone for the building was laid in November acceleration, speed and hard ride. (Aviation and 1856 and it finally disappeared from the scene Transport/ S N J White/R Marshall) in 1960. (Aviation and Transport/S N J White)

⟶ 14. This view depicts one of the fine Grimsby six wheeled AECs, namely 11, also completing the same manoeuvre on the short working to High Cliff in Cleethorpes. When these vehicles were new they had platform doors but these were later removed giving free access to the central split staircase. The 1929 shop to the rear has had another change of ownership. (H Luff/Online Transport Archive/Photobus)

15.　　Cleethorpes BUT 62 (now 162) moves round the sharp curve to the north west side of the Old Market Place on the last day of trolleybus operation on 4th June 1960. The side elevation of this batch of vehicles with Northern Coach Builders (NCB) bodywork had quite an austere appearance and the side route indicator has been painted over. The coat of arms of each municipality can be seen. A Lincolnshire Road Car Bristol MW brings up the rear on the recently introduced Route 45 to Immingham.
(J S King)

━━━▶ 16.　　Grimsby utility Karrier W 2 has completed the movement to the north west side of the Old Market Place and stands outside the large building that was once Turner's Drapery Store in August 1952. Part of the building has been taken over by the Ministry of Food as a Registration Office, which will bring back memories to older generations of immediate post war food rationing.
(R Marshall)

━━━▶ 17.　　On a very wet day in May 1957 Cleethorpes BUT 59 (now 159) awaits an early evening departure to its home town. Although in joint ownership, and having had 100 added to the fleet number in Cleethorpes style numerals, it is still in the municipality's grey and blue livery.
(J Copland/C Routh)

18.   In the period immediately after the war Cleethorpes AEC 57 is seen on the north west side of the Old Market Place; it is picking up passengers next to the Food Office referred to earlier. 57 will leave the scene top centre, turn right into Victoria Street West and complete the single line loop when it rejoins double overhead at George Street. Only the tower of the Corn Exchange remains which, as already mentioned, disappeared in 1960. (Commercial postcard. Author's collection)

21 November 1936

CHANGE OVER IN TRANSPORT

NEW TROLLEY BUSES TO-MORROW

TRAMS BETWEEN RIBY SQ. AND CLEETHORPES

TO-MORROW sees the introduction of a fresh traffic system in Grimsby, for the change over from trams, in this instance, involves more than the mere substitution of trolley vehicles.

Eventually the trolley vehicles will run right through from the Old Market-place to Cleethorpes, where it is intended that the terminus shall be at the Bathing Pool, instead of the present tram terminus.

For the present, however, the trolley buses will run only from Old Market to Park-street, and, of course, Freeman-street and Hainton-avenue as at present.

Pending the carrying out of the conversion to the trolley system at Cleethorpes, the tram service from Riby-square to Cleethorpes will continue as at present.

GRIMSBY –
VICTORIA STREETS

19.   With the Hope and Anchor pub in the background Grimsby AEC 17 makes its way along Victoria Street South near Pasture Street and will shortly turn left into George Street at the beginning of the single line loop to the Grimsby terminus. Other businesses on view in this June 1955 scene are L G Stanton, Grocers and the premises of R Kitchen. (J C Gillham)

◄———— 20. Grimsby AEC 17 is seen again this time rounding the bend in Victoria Street South with a second vehicle from the same batch in the distance and parked almost opposite the Grimsby garage. The traction standards in the foreground both carry trolleybus request stops and the maltings building on the left is unusual, given the fourth and fifth floor hoist bay construction. (S Letts)

◄———— 21. Grimsby AEC 14 picks up at the request stop outside the Grimsby garage in Victoria Street South on the inward journey to Old Market Place. The tramway offices can be seen on the left with the 1928 year of construction clearly indicated; the building no longer exists. The overhead turnout and crossover for the wiring into the garage can be seen as a Series 1 Morris 8 car overtakes and a Jaguar saloon plus a Ford V8 make their way towards the docks. (R F Mack/copyright J Fozard)

22.   At the same location another Grimsby AEC, namely 11, overtakes a family outing in an otherwise deserted street. Does anyone in the Grimsby area recognise the family on the bicycles? (R F Mack/copyright J Fozard)

23. In virtually the same location Grimsby AEC 16 passes the garage in June 1953, with the property to the rear yet to be demolished to make way for the new Grimsby police station. Before the station was built the waste ground opposite the garage was used as a parking area for Grimsby motorbuses.
(John H Meredith)

24. Cleethorpes AEC 52 is seen passing the Grimsby motorbus parking area in August 1950 and on the extreme right is an example of the rare pre-war revolutionary AEC Q type motorbus (48), that had a set back front axle and side mounted engine. Equally interesting is the AEC Regent (38) parked next to it. It was Grimsby's first double decker being fitted with a central entrance/staircase, which was jointly patented by the bodybuilder Roe, and the Corporation's Manager J.C.Whitely. The vehicle suffered wartime damage and received a new utility style body.
(D F Parker)

25. Immaculately turned out Cleethorpes AEC 55, possibly just out of the paint shop, makes its way along Victoria Street South to the Old Market Place with the Grimsby police station under construction to the rear of the Standard 14 saloon. Yet another ventilation louvre pattern can be seen in the front inspection panel this time with only six louvres.
(S H Jackson/R F Mack)

26. The same location has ———→ 27. Cleethorpes AEC 54 (now 154) in Cleethorpes BUT 61 (now 161) in joint joint ownership, but still in Cleethorpes livery, is seen ownership on what appears to be a crew travelling in the opposite direction, having overtaken change. The police station to the right ex Grimsby AEC Regal single deck motorbus 66. The has been completed and the overhead garage front can be seen on the right together with the turnout into the garage can be seen to overhead crossovers from the two doorways leading the rear. The influence of Eastern Coach to and from the southern wiring. Presumably vehicles Works design can be clearly seen in the entering or leaving the garage in the northerly direction NCB body style. (R G H Simpson) required a boom changeover. (J Fozard)

———→ 28. In September 1952 a sparkling Grimsby utility Karrier W 3 appears to be virtually full and those in the waiting queue will soon hear the conductor's shout of "only eight standing" as he gives the driver four bells. The location is Victoria Street South adjacent to Central Market on the right. Older generations will recall the Gold Flake cigarette brand advertised on the hoarding. (J Copland/C Routh)

29.   At the same location Grimsby Karrier W 24 passes the ten-table Billiard Hall with the Central Market Post Office to the rear. With today's attitudes on smoking it is doubtful that the use of Capstan cigarettes would help one to make friends as suggested by the between decks advertisement. The view dates from June 1952. (S N J White/R Marshall)

⟶   30. Immaculately turned out Cleethorpes Crossley 63 leaves Victoria Street North and enters Victoria Street South in June 1953 with Central Market on the right fronted by Chapman's Hotel. To the rear is the Palace Snack Bar taking its name from the theatre on the opposite side of the road. Note the Series 1 Morris 8 car on the right. (John H Meredith)

⟶ 31. On the opposite side of the road the now demolished Palace Theatre in Victoria Street North provides the backdrop for Grimsby utility Karrier W 3 on its way to Cleethorpes in April 1954. To the left of the theatre was the Palace Buffet which was not destroyed and is now refurbished as a Car Phone Warehouse outlet. (D F Parker)

32.   Grimsby AEC 18 puts in an appearance with Cleethorpes BUT 62 behind in Victoria Street North; both are inward bound to the Old Market Place. In the background is the Globe Cinema whose double seats older generations may well remember from their courting days.
(Roy Brook)

GRIMSBY CORPORATION TRANSPORT

TRAMWAY   SERVICE

ON and after Sunday, 22nd November, 1936, THE SERVICE OF TRAM-CARS between Old Market Place and Riby Square WILL BE WITHDRAWN.
    These will be SUBSTITUTED BY A SERVICE OF TROLLEY BUSES operating between the Old Market Place and Park Street. Until further notice the service of Tramcars between Riby Square and the Kingsway, Cleethorpes, will continue to operate as heretofore.
            J. C. WHITELEY,
    General Manager and Engineer.
19th November, 1936.

21 November 1936

GRIMSBY –
CLEETHORPE ROAD/RIBY SQUARE

33.   This April 1959 view depicts the double level crossing at Cleethorpe Road Junction with Cleethorpes Crossley 64 (now 164) in joint ownership making its way to the Old Market Place. This crossing was a source of frequent traffic hold-ups (said to be one of the busiest in the country at its peak) and played havoc with schedules; presumably the railway employed policeman with point duty armlets awaits the next interruption to traffic flow. A road bridge was constructed to overcome this problem leading from Riby Square in the background although subsequently rail activity reduced with the decline of the fishing industry. The sunblinds over the signal box windows are a novel feature. (D F Parker)

34. Also seen moving across the railway crossing in May 1957 is Cleethorpes AEC 58 (now 158) in joint ownership but still in its municipal livery. The signal box controlling the railway junction and crossing is again in view with the multi-storey cold storage building in the far distance and the Dock Offices on the left. The advertisement on the wall in front of the signal box is promoting Holiday Runabout tickets at twenty-two shillings and sixpence each (112.5p). (J Copland/ C Routh)

35. Grimsby AEC 12 is seen in Cleethorpe Road passing Halifax House, now the local offices of the Transport and General Workers Union, and is about to reach Riby Square. On the left is the Midland Bank building with the upper floors housing Lloyds Register of Shipping reflecting Grimsby's port activities. There was no wiring from this direction into Riby Square so trolleybuses taking up service on Route 10 to Weelsby Road had to manually transfer booms; this was repeated when coming off service. (D A Jones/London Trolleybus Preservation Society)

36.   We now arrive at Riby Square which was the town terminus for the opening Grimsby trolleybus route to Weelsby Road and also the short workings from the Cleethorpes direction. Cleethorpes AEC 53, in original dark blue livery, awaits departure back to the Bathing Pool having turned round in the Square. The damaged front panel is in need of attention. (R F Mack/J Fozard copyright)

37. At the same location two Grimsby vehicles wait outside the National Provincial Bank (now an accountancy practice) that still has "Lincoln Bank Grimsby Fish Dock Branch" over the entrance. In the foreground is utility Park Royal bodied Karrier W 1 on Route 10 to Weelsby Road whilst to the rear is a post-war Roe bodied Karrier W. The cast iron bollard in the foreground is an attractive item of street furniture. (R F Mack/J Fozard copyright)

———➤ 38. On what appears to be a very warm day Grimsby AEC 15 leaves Riby Square and moves across Cleethorpe Road to enter Freeman Street on its way to Weelsby Road. An overhead triangular crossover can be seen in the top of the picture. Note the small fleet number on the front panel, as in the previous view, and the gentleman leaning on the railings who also appears in the next view.
(R F Mack/J Fozard copyright)

———➤ 39. This view depicts the Riby Square turning circle with wiring from Cleethorpe Road coming in from the right; the wiring on the left leading into the Square is from Freeman Street. Cleethorpes AEC 57 hurries across the junction and is about to pass under the crossover as it continues along Cleethorpe Road with the premises of Consolidated Fisheries Limited in the background. (A D Packer)

40.   Cleethorpes BUT 60 (now 160) in joint ownership passes Riby Square on the left as it moves along Cleethorpe Road with the female cyclist moving across the end of Freeman Street in June 1960. The clock above the police box indicates it is mid afternoon as 160 is followed by AEC Regent V motorbus 106 with the overhead turnout for Riby Square turning circle immediately above. (J C Gillham)

41. Grimsby Karrier W 2 with utility Park Royal bodywork is seen in Cleethorpe Road just beyond Riby Square which is round the corner from the National Provincial Bank. This utility design of bodywork was supplied to many trolleybus operators towards the end and immediately after the 1939-45 war. (J C Gillham)

42. This rather blurred view of an unidentified Grimsby AEC six wheeler hurrying along Cleethorpe Road has been included as it depicts the original livery, which had a greater expanse of cream, and the central entrance folding doors. The view was probably taken not long after the conversion from trams to trolleybuses in 1936, as tram track and overhead are still in place and a coil of suspension wire can be seen hanging from the out of view traction standard on the right. The location is adjacent to Stanley Street with the Ebenezer Primitive Methodist Chapel beyond the trolleybus; the building later became the New Clee Methodist Chapel and is now the site of the Toy & Sports Department of the Ramsden Superstore, having previously been an Asda store after the demolition of the chapel. (Courtesy of the Grimsby Evening Telegraph)

43.   Ex Cleethorpes BUT 62 (now 162) has crossed the boundary between the two towns at Park Street having left Grimsby Road, Cleethorpes and entered Cleethorpe Road, Grimsby. The Park Street short working overhead wiring can be seen on the right with each operator having its own "round the houses" loop back towards their home territory. Ex Grimsby AEC Regent III motorbus 82 travels in the opposite direction on trolleybus Route 11 to Cleethorpes on 4th June 1960, which was the last day of trolleybus operation. (J Copland/C Routh)

GRIMSBY -
FREEMAN STREET, HAINTON AVENUE & WEELSBY ROAD

44.   Returning to Riby Square we now follow Grimsby's opening 1926 trolleybus route along Freeman Street and Hainton Avenue to Weelsby Road, known as 'The Alley' by the crews, which was the domain of the Garrett single deckers. This view taken circa 1945 shows Garrett 3 (renumbered 5 in 1944) on the west side of Riby Square waiting to turn round ready for the return trip to the suburbs. Pre-war photographs of this vehicle show it illuminated with "Adapt and Improve" on one side and "Progress and Prosperity" on the other. The display was to mark the reinstatement of Freeman Street after the lifting of the tram track, the latter having had an adverse affect on the many tradesmen along this thoroughfare. (A Tye collection)

Trolley Vehicles.

ORDINARY SERVICE.

	Interval of Service.	WEEKDAYS		SUNDAYS.	
		First a.m.	Last p.m.	First p.m.	Last p.m.
	Mins.				
Riby Square to Weelsby Road	10	5 10	—	—	—
Riby Square to Weelsby Road	5	6 40	11 10	1 50	11 10
Weelsby Road to Riby Square	10	5 20	—	—	—
Weelsby Road to Riby Square	5	6 50	11 20	2 0	11 20

The Ordinary Services are supplemented by Special Vehicles at rush hours.

Timetable 1928

45.　　This rear view of Garrett 1 depicts a busy scene at the end of Freeman Street with the 18" (457mm) wide spaced overhead curving into the terminal loop in Riby Square. The shoe shop on the right is interesting with what appear to be thigh length boots on display (probably for fishermen) together with external lighting to illuminate the window display during the hours of darkness. The gentleman with a bowler hat in the foreground gives a whole new meaning to the word "manpower". (A Tye collection)

46.   This second rear view at the bottom end of Freeman Street depicts single decker Garrett 7 making its way towards Riby Square that is in the distance. This is a scene full of atmosphere with a wide variety of shops, horse-drawn drays, a window cleaner's barrow and numerous unattended bicycles. Most of the overhead wiring seems to have been altered to a wider spacing than the 18" (457mm) seen in the previous view. Initially the Garretts travelled from the garage in Victoria Street South to take up service at Riby Square using a trailing skate in the tram track with the conductor walking behind to ensure it remained engaged.
(Courtesy of Grimsby Evening Telegraph)

47.   The mystery photograph. Following the opening of the first Grimsby trolleybus route to Weelsby Road with five Garrett vehicles traffic was disrupted whilst tram track was lifted and consequently headways increased. It is reported that an additional vehicle was loaned from Ipswich for a few months until a further two Garretts were delivered. This photograph of Ipswich Ransomes single decker 15 in Freeman Street would seem to confirm this report although no evidence can be found back at Ipswich. However, the view has a "doctored" feel about it, especially the position of the cyclist on the left who seems to be floating off the ground; the shadow of the trolleybus also seems wrong. A further report indicated an Ipswich trolleybus was hired some time during the 1939-45 war, although again there is no evidence in Ipswich records. Any confirmation of these reports would be appreciated.
(Commercial postcard. Author's collection)

GRIMSBY.

The Grimsby Corporation Tramways operate one route of 1½ miles by a fleet **of 7 Garrett Electric Trolley Buses** and a 5 minute service is maintained by utilising 6 buses during the rush-hour periods and 4 buses during ordinary periods. The route is practically level but there are several dangerous cross-streets, which are negotiated safely.

The number of passengers carried for the year 1927/1928 was 3,344,358, **and the current consumption 1.41 units per bus mile.** Another interesting comparison with former tramway services is provided in this instance. The same route was previously operated by 5 tramcars but since then **the length of the route has been increased nearly 50%** and the same route is served now by **4 Trolley Buses in place of the former 5 tramcars,** and the time taken for return journey over the longer route **is 20 minutes as compared with the time taken by the tramcars over the shorter route of 25 minutes.**

48.   Views of the Grimsby Garrett single deckers are rare hence the inclusion of this crash scene in Freeman Street at the junction with Wellington Street that occurred on 23rd April 1928. The driver of the Garrett swerved to miss a runaway horse and entered the shop of Horsewood & Co, rabbit and poultry dealer. The group surrounding it includes two bowler-hatted gentlemen, who are presumably discussing how to extricate the vehicle, whilst the policeman ensures the road is kept clear. Note the single mounting for the booms and that the spare wheel is missing from its carrier. (Courtesy of the Grimsby Evening Telegraph)

49.   Grimsby Karrier W 23 has almost reached the terminus at Weelsby Road in May 1952 and will stop to unload passengers before turning round for the return trip to Riby Square. The between wars suburban housing forms the backdrop with Rialto Avenue leading off Hainton Avenue on the left. This road, and others nearby, are named after Grimsby trawlers and it would have formed the first leg of a "round the houses" turning manoeuvre if there had not been objections from residents. (A D Packer)

50.   An unidentified Garrett turns back for town at Weelsby Road. It is reported that when this route was opened, the turning manoeuvre required a red flag to be carried in front of the vehicle and this view may well be illustrating this activity as the conductor is certainly in the roadway with an object in his left hand. (E N Osborne/Online Transport Archive)

51.   This unidentified Grimsby AEC six wheeler has nearly completed the turning manoeuvre and is about to move into Hainton Avenue with Weelsby Road in the background. As can be seen the junction was controlled by traffic lights and contacts on the overhead wiring allowed the trolleybus to sequence the lights to provide a safe manoeuvre. The contact to return the lighting sequence to normal can just be seen above the front of the vehicle. (G Warnes)

52.   This view shows Grimsby Karrier W 19 waiting to return to Riby Square having completed the manoeuvre around the turning circle and with the destination indicator unchanged. Note the stop sign and the overhead contact on the left leading into the circle which controlled the traffic lights in favour of the trolleybus. In the late 1940's a driver approaching the terminus in the early hours of the morning fell asleep and sped straight across the road junction into the field beyond the fence. (C Routh)

CLEETHORPES -
GRIMSBY AND PELHAM ROADS

53.   Grimsby Karrier W 21 in joint ownership leaves Grimsby Road and is about to pass the boundary between the two towns on its way to the Old Market Place in May 1960. The wiring leading to the right from the overhead junction is the "round the houses" short working turning loop from the Cleethorpes direction which lead into Park Street and then ran along Sidney Street and Daubney Street before rejoining Grimsby Road in the far distance. The wiring entering from the extreme right is the end of the Grimsby loop. Note the section insulators on both sets of negative and positive overhead wiring; they were presumably installed to segregate the electricity supplies when there were two separate undertakings. (J C Gillham)

54.   Another view of the boundary between the two towns looking along Grimsby Road with Cleethorpes Crossley 64 (now 164) about to negotiate the overhead junctions for Park Street on the last day of operation on 4th June 1960. The end of the Grimsby short working "round the houses" loop is in the foreground having travelled via Rutland and Hamilton Streets and the entrance to the similar Cleethorpes short working loop is beyond. The Clee Park Hotel on the left is now a car park.
(J S King)

(top right)
55.   In this September 1959 view we are looking along Park Street, the boundary between the two towns, with Grimsby Karrier W 24 in joint ownership leaving Grimsby Road, Cleethorpes and about to enter Cleethorpe Road, Grimsby. In the centre of the view the short working "round the houses" loops can be seen with the Cleethorpes wiring on the left leading from Park Street into Sidney Street. Grimsby wiring exits from Hamilton Street on the right into Park Street. On the main line wiring the section insulators can be seen again on all four sets of wiring which segregated the two electrical supplies. (J H Price)

56. This Grimsby Road view of Cleethorpes Crossley 64 taken in June 1956 has been included to illustrate the overhead wiring leading into Pelham Road and thence to the Cleethorpes depot (Note the Grimsby term 'Garage' was not used, although some destination blinds did indicate 'Depot'). Access to and from Pelham Road could be achieved from either direction and a driver travelling towards Cleethorpes required skill to negotiate the dead sections in the overhead fittings. (A D Packer)

57. Cleethorpes AEC 53 ——→ 58. In almost the same location Cleethorpes AEC 56 from the original batch of is seen in the later blue and grey livery in July 1953. Although trolleybuses, and in the first dark from the same batch as the vehicle in the previous view, 56 has blue livery, is seen in Pelham been refurbished with sliding windows in place of half-drops, Road parked opposite the depot rain shields removed and the upper deck front windows replaced in August 1948. The house to with fixed panes. For a period in the early 1950's this vehicle the rear no longer exists. (and possibly 57) was decorated with coloured lights. (R Marshall) (R Marshall)

——→ 59. In this view we see Cleethorpes 62 in the original dark blue livery parked under the exit wiring from the depot on the right in the early months of the 1939-45 war. Interestingly a headlight mask is fitted to the offside but there are no other wartime features that were usually added to deal with the blackout. In view of reduced wartime passenger loadings this vehicle, together with 59 to 61, were sold to Nottingham City Transport in 1940 becoming their 437 to 440. (R Marshall collection)

(left) 60. The lower part of Pelham Road and the depot area, seen here in August 1952, are unrecognisable today, being now covered by a large cold storage facility. Parked on the exit wiring from the depot, that leads to Grimsby Road, are two Cleethorpes BUT trolleybuses with 60 in the foreground. The influence of Eastern Coach Works bodywork style is again evident. (R Marshall)

(lower left) 61. This view was taken on the last day of trolleybus operation on 4th June 1960 and depicts Cleethorpes Crossley 64 (now 164) at the end of Grimsby Road and about to overtake ex-Grimsby rebodied Guy Arab II motorbus 78 before climbing Isaacs Hill into Cleethorpes town centre. The Guy is showing Route 11 and Grimsby Old Market Place, so presumably it will turn back at the roundabout at the bottom of Isaacs Hill that is a short distance further on. Today a water tower replaces the chimney stack on the skyline. (J Copland)

CLEETHORPES -
ISAACS HILL/HIGH STREET

62. Also on the last day of operation Cleethorpes Crossley 64 (now 164) has dropped down Isaacs Hill and rounds the roundabout to enter Grimsby Road. The short working wiring from Grimsby, erected in 1957 to replace the facility lost when Pelham Road depot closed, comes in from the left and the Jowett Javelin car is parked outside properties that are now mainly boarding houses. (J S King)

63. The short working wiring indicated in the previous picture is just off to the left of this view as Grimsby Karrier W 19 in joint ownership climbs Isaacs Hill and thence to Cleethorpes High Street. The traction standards appear to be receiving a re-paint or a two-tone colour scheme existed. (D Tate)

→ 64. In this August 1952 view we see a typical seaside day and, although the open windscreen would seem to indicate a high temperature, many of the public have their topcoats on. Grimsby AEC 12 loads at the end of Cleethorpes High Street ready for the return to its home town with a Cleethorpes Willowbrook bodied Daimler motorbus destined for Park Street following behind. The coat of arms is under the rear staircase window on this trolleybus. (R Marshall)

→ 65. Two of the Grimsby utility Park Royal bodied Karrier W's pass on a typical summer's day at the end of Cleethorpes High Street in July 1953. 1 on the left will soon turn right into Alexandra Road and thence travel above the promenade, whilst 3 will continue along the High Street and then drop down Isaacs Hill. The area to the right is now occupied by a row of single storey shops. (R Marshall)

66.   On a warm summer's day in July 1953 Cleethorpes AEC 55 gets ready for the return to Grimsby as it picks up passengers at the end of Cleethorpes High Street. The curve of overhead wiring from the sea front area in Alexandra Road can be seen in the background as a conductor collects fares from the queuing crowds. This arrangement was used to ensure all fares were collected from passengers returning from the beach and the attractions of the sea front. (R Marshall)

67.   Also at the same location Grimsby Karrier W 23 prepares to return to the Old Market Place, whilst people make their way back from the pleasures of the beach and the pier in August 1952. Other visitors will return to their homes farther afield by train from Cleethorpes railway station that is adjacent to the beach and a few hundred yards to the left of this view. (R Marshall)

68.   On the opposite side of High Street Grimsby AEC 12 is about to turn into Alexandra Road and travel above the Cleethorpes sea front in May 1954. The Bazaar, which is now Mitchell's Bar, seems to be popular and the use of a domestic property as a snack bar is unusual. (D F Parker)

69.   At the same location Cleethorpes AEC 50 is seen in original dark blue livery in June 1950 with the replacement rear panel yet to be painted. In the previous view comment was made about the domestic property used as a snack bar, but next door has gone one better as a fish and chip café. (S Letts)

CLEETHORPES -
ALEXANDRA ROAD

70.   Grimsby Karrier W 19 in joint ownership has just left Cleethorpes High Street and is at the end of Alexandra Road ready to move off towards High Cliff and onwards to the Bathing Pool in September 1959. The Victoria Hotel seen in the background is now an O'Neill's bar, although a separate building behind the hedge still has wording over the doorway indicating that it was the Victoria Hotel Garage. (A B Cross)

71.   Cleethorpes BUT 60 (now 160) in joint ownership is about to enter the curve leading from Alexandra Road into Cleethorpes High Street. To the left are the gardens above the promenade and pier. The span wire at the top of the view is clearly in need of tensioning. (D Tate/R F Mack/ National Trolleybus Association Collection)

72.   Cleethorpes Crossley 64 passes the Dolphin Hotel, now the Reflex/Flares bar and nightclub, and is about to leave Alexandra Road for Cleethorpes High Street. Additional twin line hangers have been inserted into the span wires to allow the overhead to be temporarily re-aligned to accommodate the on-going roadworks in June 1956. (J Copland/C Routh)

(left) 73. Grimsby AEC 14 passes the roadworks in Alexandra Road with the High Cliff short working terminus in the far distance. The Pier Gardens above the promenade are on the left and what could well be taken as traction standards are still in place today along this stretch of road to provide support for illuminations. (R F Mack/copyright J Fozard)

(lower left) 74. Cleethorpes BUT 59 hurries along Alexandra Road in August 1956 with a destination blind suggesting the vehicle will turn a little further on at High Cliff and return to Pelham Road Depot. Fairy lights are strung between the traction standards above the flowerbeds in full bloom and against the backdrop of shops that are little changed today, although the building on the left no longer exists and is now the site of the local library. (S Letts)

CLEETHORPES -
HIGH CLIFF

75. We now arrive at the High Cliff short working terminus from the Grimsby direction where trolleybuses servicing Cleethorpes High Street and the popular sea front area turned back. Here Grimsby utility Karrier W 3, looking as if it has just left the paint shop, arrives at the terminus with Grimsby AEC 17 behind carrying a full load for the Bathing Pool and about to be overtaken by a Morris 10 saloon. (C Carter)

76.   Cleethorpes BUT 62 begins the turn around the High Cliff roundabout ready for the return towards Grimsby in June 1956. The building to the rear now houses the offices of the North East Lincolnshire Council. (J C Gillham)

77.   Cleethorpes AEC 54 is seen part way round the terminal wiring in June 1956 having passed under the crossover and parked outside the High Cliff Hotel; this was the location for early interviews for North Sea rig workers. The hotel is now demolished and apartments were being built on the site at the time of writing. (J C Gillham)

78.   Almost at the same location Cleethorpes AEC 52 leaves High Cliff Road and is about to pass under the wooden insulated terminus crossover. The rear of a Morris Commercial van can just be seen on the right. (C Carter)

79.   Cleethorpes AEC 55, in original dark blue livery, and looking the worse for wear, rounds the curve from High Cliff Road in the immediate post-war period and is about to move round the roundabout that formed the High Cliff short working terminus. A Grimsby utility Karrier W waits to complete the turn back whilst an inspector talks to the crew. (A D Packer)

80.   Cleethorpes BUT 62, with the destination display showing, will turn short at Riby Square on its return to Grimsby. The High Cliff terminus was where High Cliff Road and Alexandra Road met at the junction with Sea View Street seen to the rear. The pub in the background continues to trade and the building to the right of 62, plus the house next door, are now a NatWest Bank. The car in the background is a Rover 14. (D A Jones/London Trolleybus Preservation Society)

81. Having completed the turning manoeuvre Grimsby Karrier W 20 waits prior to the return to Grimsby. The destination display has still to be changed and the route number box indicates "Relief Bus". The shop on the right is now an Indian restaurant and on the left can be seen the rear of an Austin 7 car. (D A Jones/ London Trolleybus Preservation Society)

82. Vehicles from both undertakings complete these scenes of the High Cliff terminus, with an immaculate Cleethorpes AEC 55 on the main line having passed Grimsby Karrier W 20 waiting at the end of the turning circle wiring. The flowerbeds are a credit to the Parks Department and the Austin 7 referred to earlier is again in view.
(D A Jones/London Trolleybus Preservation Society)

CLEETHORPES -
HIGH CLIFF ROAD/KINGSWAY

83.   We now leave the High Cliff terminus, which is just beyond the curve on the left, as Cleethorpes BUT 60 (now 160) in joint ownership enters High Cliff Road in the summer of 1957 with the Humber estuary on the right. 160 still carries the Cleethorpes livery. The pavilion immediately to the rear is the one that can be seen in Picture 78. (J Copland/D F Parker)

⟶ 84. Grimsby Karrier W 23 leaves High Cliff Road in August 1956 under bracket arm suspended overhead wiring and is about to enter Kingsway on the last stage of its journey to the Bathing Pool. In the background the road rises to the site of the High Cliff terminus and the slipway drops down to the beach to the right of the policeman. Ye Olde Barn Tea House, which is now Willy's Bar and Brewery, is on the corner of Brighton Street. (S Letts)

⟶ 85. Further along Kingsway Cleethorpes Crossley 63 and AEC 58 pass each other adjacent to Segmere Street on the left. In the far distance the incline of High Cliff Road can be seen leading up to the short working terminus referred to earlier. The ground floor of the building on the left is now the Café Valerie. (R F Mack/copyright J Fozard)

86.   On the last day of trolleybus operation Grimsby Karrier W 19 moves along Kingsway on the final leg of the journey to Cleethorpes Bathing Pool. There are shelters along Kingsway as seen in the left background; the roofs are unchanged but the areas below have been redesigned. The garden area beyond the railings was to be used for a proposed extension of the tramway from the final terminus at the far end of Kingsway. Note the Riley RM Series car on the left and the Austin Westminster A90 on the right. (J S King)

——————▶ 87. Cleethorpes Crossley 63 has just left the Bathing Pool in the background on the return trip to Grimsby with the now demolished dancing establishment Café Dansant on the left. Perhaps a sign of the 1950's is the number of motorcycles, some with sidecars, which provided many working class families with independent transport before the growth of post-war car ownership. (R F Mack)

——————▶ 88. Cleethorpes Crossley 64 (now 164) in joint ownership at the end of the journey to the Bathing Pool in September 1959 approaches the turning circle, with the overhead wiring along the Kingsway extension stretching into the distance towards the bottom of High Cliff Road. The Café Dansant can be seen again on the right with forthcoming attractions including a weekly dancing programme plus harmony and café nights. (M Dryhurst)

CLEETHORPES – BATHING POOL

89.   We arrive at the Cleethorpes Bathing Pool terminus in this view taken in June 1956. The turning facility was created with the opening of the Cleethorpes section of the system in July 1937 when traffic flows were light, but in later years this area could become quite congested. On view are a Grimsby Roe bodied Karrier W plus Cleethorpes' Crossley 64 and AEC 55 on the right with a Series 2 Morris 8 car moving towards the photographer and a Flying Standard 16 travelling in the opposite direction. (J S King)

──────────→ 90. In June 1956 vehicles from both municipalities are seen in this view with the Café Dansant in the background and the rear of a Standard Vanguard car between them. In the foreground is Cleethorpes AEC 55 followed by Grimsby Karrier W 20.
(J Copland/C Routh)

──────────→ 91. Waiting to turn for the return trip to Grimsby in September 1959 is that municipality's Karrier W 19 in joint ownership with the Café Dansant and Bathing Pool entrance as background. (M Dryhurst)

92.   Grimsby Karrier W 23 is seen at the Bathing Pool in August 1948 seventeen months after delivery and in original livery with a greater expanse of cream around the lower deck windows and three bands of lining out. Subsequent repaints saw the lower deck cream area reduced to just above the windows terminating in front of the staircase glazing. (R Marshall)

⟶ 93. Also waiting to turn is Cleethorpes AEC 50 in original dark blue livery. The vehicle still has the original half-drop side windows and front window ventilators. The former were replaced with sliding versions and the latter removed on many of these pre-war vehicles. The absence of people at 3.40pm suggests a winter scene. (W J Haynes)

⟶ 94. Cleethorpes AEC 55 begins the turning manoeuvre; when the route opened in July 1937 white road markings were provided to help drivers gain the correct position under the overhead for the turn. This was the last of the Cleethorpes AEC's to be withdrawn (1959) and was the only pre war trolleybus from either fleet to be painted in the joint ownership livery. (H Luff/Online Transport Archive/Photobus)

95.   Half way round the turning circle Cleethorpes Crossley 64 will complete the manoeuvre to pick up passengers for the return trip to Grimsby. The conductor still has to change the side route indicator and in the background a Rover saloon can be seen. (C Carter)

———→ 96. Cleethorpes AEC 54, in original dark blue livery, completes the Bathing Pool turn with the steps of this open-air facility in view; a far cry from today's modern Leisure Centre on the same site. The dual carriageway of Kings Road beyond seems ideal for trolleybus operation but it was not to be. (Commercial postcard. Author's collection)

———→ 97. The cycling policeman overtakes an immaculate Cleethorpes AEC 54 as the evening sunshine casts long shadows across the road. The turn back has been completed with Cromwell Road leading off to the right. Note the ornamental cast iron base for the traction standard on the right; the standard to the rear of the policeman is still in place at the time of writing. (J Fozard)

98.	In August 1952 two Cleethorpes BUT trolleybuses can be seen, with 61 in the foreground carrying a fair loading for the short working to Park Street. It would be interesting to know the reason for specifying the requirement for a small nearside cab sliding window (no door) on Cleethorpes vehicles. (R Marshall)

99.	A rear view of Grimsby AEC 11 shows it departing for the return trip to Grimsby in May 1956. The design of the boom retainer is of interest with inward facing hooks that prevented side movement when lowering into the final location. The position of the rear wheels relative to the central entrance meant that anyone jumping onto the open platform whilst the bus was in motion was in great danger of severe injury if they missed their footing. (R F Mack/ National Trolleybus Association)

DEPOTS

100.   Grimsby garage is seen in its heyday with utility Karrier W 1 on the left next to pre-war AEC 12. The steel work for the building originated from an ex-World War I Admiralty seaplane hanger that was for sale in the early 1920's and located at Killingholme near Immingham. Grimsby purchased the building in 1925 and used the framework as the basic structure to provide a facility for their recently purchased trams from the Great Grimsby Street Tramways Company. Contracts were placed for the rest of the building work with construction being completed in 1926, although the date on the front of the building indicating 1925 was the year of the Corporation takeover. The building is still in use today. During the period of construction the Grimsby trams continued to operate out of the company's depot in Pelham Road, Cleethorpes. (K W Moody/R Marshall)

101. In this view representatives from both towns' fleets are seen inside Grimsby garage in July 1958. On the left is Cleethorpes Crossley 63 (now 163) standing next to Grimsby Karrier W 24, both in joint ownership, and both fitted with Roe bodywork. Tram track is still in evidence and much of the overhead equipment in the garage was rescued by the London Trolleybus Preservation Society after closure and used at the East Anglian Transport Museum, Carlton Colville, Suffolk. (D F Parker)

102 Cleethorpes AEC 58 leaves its home Pelham Road Depot to travel the short distance to Grimsby Road complete with an advertisement for a local baker. The entrance wiring can just be seen on the left of the upper deck window and evidence of earlier tram track can be seen bottom left. The depot was built by the local firm of Wilkinson and Houghton for the opening of the company's electric tram operations. It closed operationally in March 1957 and was sold in 1958. (Norman J Drewry)

ROLLING STOCK - GRIMSBY

1926 1-5 EE6461-5   **Garrett O**
1927 6-7 EE7097-8   **Garrett O**

103.   These were the single deck vehicles acquired for the first tram to trolleybus conversion of the Freeman Street/Hainton Avenue route with its extension to Weelsby Road. They were fitted with Bull 50hp motors and Roe central entrance bodies with 36 seats. The first withdrawal was in 1939 and the last to go was 6 in 1946. 3 was renumbered 5 in 1944 to make way for the wartime Karrier deliveries. 2 is seen at an unidentified location displaying body builder's advertising.
(J S Bullen (Grimsby)/R Marshall)

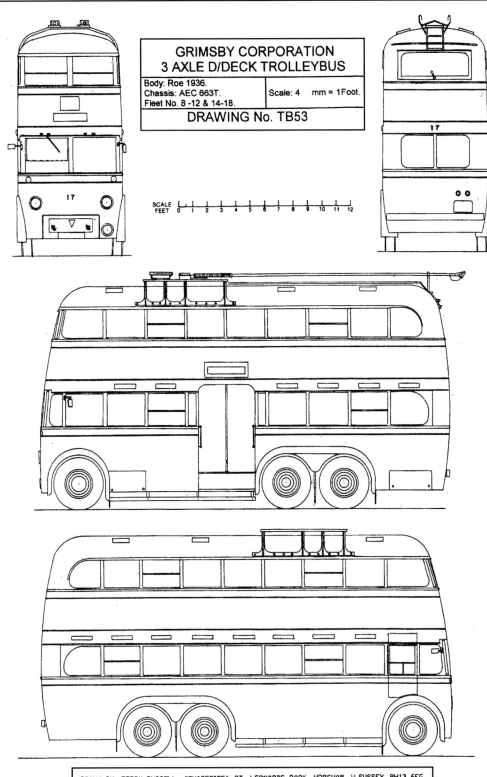

GRIMSBY CORPORATION
3 AXLE D/DECK TROLLEYBUS

Body: Roe 1936.
Chassis: AEC 663T.
Fleet No. 8 -12 & 14-18.

Scale: 4 mm = 1Foot.

DRAWING No. TB53

17

SCALE
FEET 0 1 2 3 4 5 6 7 8 9 10 11 12

17

DRAWN BY:—TERRY RUSSELL, "CHACESIDE", ST. LEONARDS PARK, HORSHAM, W.SUSSEX. RH13 6EG.
SEND 4 FIRST CLASS STAMPS FOR COMPLETE LIST OF PUBLIC TRANSPORT DRAWINGS.

1936   **8-12   JV5001-5   AEC 663T**
         14-18   JV5007-10/6   AEC 663T

104.   This batch of double deckers was used to convert the main route from Old Market Place to the borough boundary at Park Street and eventually to Cleethorpes. They were the last of this model for a UK customer and were fitted with 80hp Metro-Vick motors. Roe bodywork was again specified with central entrance and split staircase; originally doors were fitted to the central entrance but were removed at a later date. 32 lower deck and 26 upper deck seats were fitted and the original livery had cream between decks as illustrated. Withdrawals took place in 1955 and 1957 with four passing into joint ownership, although they may not have seen service. 18, originally intended as 13, is seen at Roe's Leeds works positioned for official photographs; note the GCT logo at the rear. (Roe)

1944 1-3 JV8701-3 Karrier W

(left) 105. These three vehicles were allocated to Grimsby during the second world war and replaced some of the remaining Garretts. They were built to a wartime Ministry specification, hence the W designation, and were produced at Sunbeam's Wolverhampton factory but badge engineered with the Karrier name. EEC 80hp motors were fitted together with Park Royal 56 seat utility bodies. All passed into joint ownership and withdrawal came in 1958. 1 is illustrated outside the Grimsby garage; note the lack of lining out below the upper deck windows. (S N J White/R Marshall)

1947 19-24 AEE 22-27 Karrier W

(lower left) 106. This batch of trolleybuses proved to be the final delivery to Grimsby and was to a wartime chassis specification but with attractive post-war Roe 56 seat bodies. Metro-Vick 85hp motors were fitted and withdrawals occurred in 1959 and 1960 with all having passed into joint ownership. After withdrawal, five were sold to Bradford City Transport for rebodying but instead they were cannibalised for spares and then sold for scrap. 21 is seen in Grimsby Old Market Place. (Aviation and Transport/S N J White)

ROLLING STOCK - CLEETHORPES

1937 50-59 FW 8986-8995 AEC 661T
1938 60-62 AFU 153-155   AEC 661T

107. These initial deliveries were fitted with Metro-Vick 80hp motors and attractive Park Royal 56 seat bodies with the first batch opening the Cleethorpes system. With the reduction in wartime passenger loadings 59-62 were sold to Nottingham City Transport in 1940 becoming their 437-440 and were eventually withdrawn in 1952. Three operational vehicles passed into joint ownership with 100 added to the fleet numbers and were withdrawn between 1957 and 1959; earlier withdrawals were between 1950 and 1954. This official body builder's photograph shows 50 in the original livery of dark blue with cream bands. The latter changed to light blue in 1939/40 and the grey livery was introduced shortly after the war. 54 is preserved at the Sandtoft Trolleybus Museum, North Lincolnshire. (Author's collection)

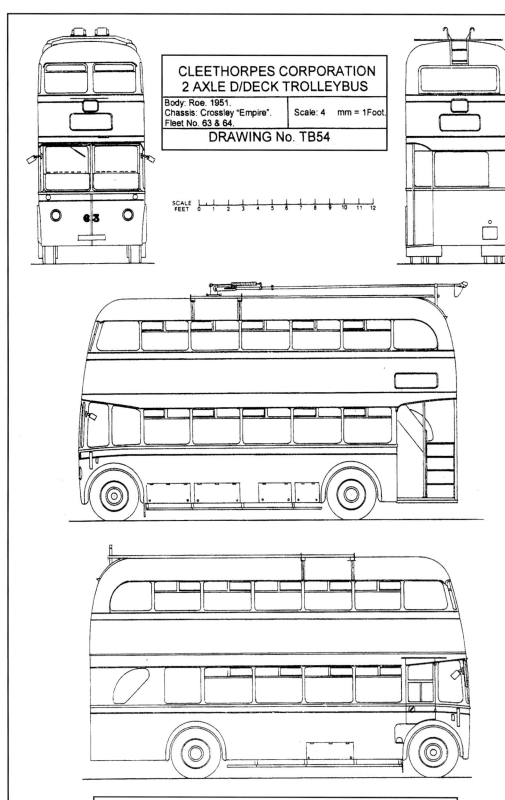

CLEETHORPES CORPORATION
2 AXLE D/DECK TROLLEYBUS

Body: Roe. 1951.
Chassis: Crossley "Empire".
Fleet No. 63 & 64.

Scale: 4 mm = 1Foot.

DRAWING No. TB54

SCALE FEET 0 1 2 3 4 5 6 7 8 9 10 11 12

DRAWN BY:-TERRY RUSSELL, "CHACESIDE", ST. LEONARDS PARK, HORSHAM, W.SUSSEX. RH13 6EG.
SEND 4 FIRST CLASS STAMPS FOR COMPLETE LIST OF PUBLIC TRANSPORT DRAWINGS.

1950 59-62 GFU692-695 BUT 9611T

108.   These were the first post-war delivery and were fitted with Metro-Vick 115hp motors and Northern Coach Builders (NCB) 54 seat bodies. The bodies bore a strong resemblance to Eastern Coach Works designs following a change of employment by a key designer. All transferred into joint ownership becoming 159-162 and were sold to Walsall Corporation in 1960 becoming their 874-877. 160-162 were lengthened by Walsall and re-built with front entrances; two had seating increased to 69 and the third to 67. When the Walsall fleet was transferred to the West Midland Passenger Transport Executive in 1969 all four came under the new ownership and were withdrawn in 1970. 59 is seen at the High Cliff short working terminus in June 1956 and is currently held at the Sandtoft Trolleybus Museum. (J C Gillham)

1951 63-64 HBE541-542 Crossley TDD42/3

109.   These two trolleybuses were the last to be delivered to Cleethorpes being fitted with Metro-Vick 95hp motors and handsome Roe 54 seat bodies. They were transferred into joint ownership becoming 163/164 and were sold to Walsall Corporation in 1960 becoming their 850/873. Both were transferred to the West Midland Passenger Transport Executive in 1969 and were withdrawn in 1970. 63 is seen at High Cliff ready to move off into High Cliff Road; its chassis was exhibited at the 1950 Commercial Motor Show. It went for preservation after withdrawal but was unfortunately scrapped later. (D A Jones/London Trolleybus Preservation Society)

◀─────── 110. This Grimsby tower wagon was converted from Albion PM28 single deck motorbus 32 delivered in 1928 and fitted with a Roe 32 seat central entrance body. It had been converted into a tower wagon by the end of 1940 and is currently privately preserved at Leadgate, Co. Durham. Others from the batch were pressed into wartime service for Fire and Health Departments. The linesman is working on the turn out junction for Grimsby garage with out of service trolleybuses in the background in May 1952. (A D Packer)

111. The Cleethorpes tower wagon was based on a Thornycroft J single decker bus new in 1910 and originally operated by the Gosport arm of the Provincial Tramways group as indicated by its AA registration letters. It was transferred to the Lincolnshire Provincial operations in 1925 and had been converted into a tower wagon by 1936. It passed into Cleethorpes ownership and was withdrawn after amalgamation. In addition, Cleethorpes withdrew their first double deck motorbus, a Leyland TD1 numbered 3, in 1950 and began its conversion into a tower wagon but the project had not been completed by the time the systems amalgamated. (J Copland)

THE BEGINNING AND THE END

112   The opening route of the Grimsby system to Weelsby Road commenced on 2nd October 1926 with five Garrett single deckers. The last of this batch (5) is seen on a return trip to Riby Square and is in Hainton Avenue near the junction with Welholme Road and with the original Congregational Mission Church in the background. Two similar vehicles were added the following year before the advent of the AEC 6 wheel double deckers for the main inter town route ten years later. Lettering on the side indicates a maximum speed of 12mph. (Garrett Long Shop Museum)

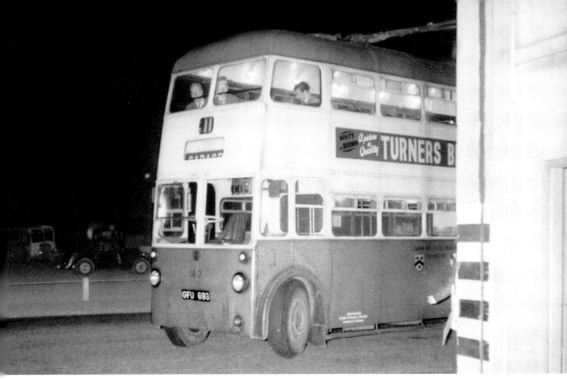

113   Having completed the very last journey from Cleethorpes 60 (now 160) has run along Victoria Street West and South from Grimsby Old Market Place and is about to enter the garage for the last time in the first hour of 5th June 1960, although the official closure date was the day before. Thus ended almost 34 years of trolleybus operation in Grimsby and all but one month of 23 years in Cleethorpes. (R F Mack)

114   Behind Grimsby garage, with the Alexandra Docks as the backdrop, two trolleybuses await disposal in June 1960 with the front inspection panels removed ready for towing away. On the right is a Cleethorpes BUT destined for Walsall Corporation and on the left a Grimsby Karrier W awaiting collection for movement to Bradford. (J Fozard)

THE AFTER LIFE

115 We move to the East Midlands in this ──────► 116. This post October 1940 September 1950 view of Cleethorpes AEC 62 in wartime view depicts ex-Cleethorpes AEC 59, the green and cream livery of Nottingham City now 437 in the Nottingham fleet, at the Vernon Transport having, been sold with three similar Road terminus. First generation overhead vehicles in 1940. 440 is seen at the Victoria equipment and trolley wheel collectors are in Embankment Trent Bridge, a regular haunt of the use and evidence of wartime conditions are author in his younger days when visiting from indicated by masked headlights, white edging, Derby, and is about to turn ready for the return black and white traction standard base, the word trip to Bulwell Market. Note the department's "Nottingham" painted out and anti-blast sticky Morris Commercial refreshment van provided tape on the windows of the end terraced house. for the benefit of staff on layover. (D F Parker) (G Atkins/R Marshall)

117.   The four Cleethorpes BUT's were sold to Walsall Corporation when the system closed and 59 (later 159) is seen here in all over blue livery turning into Wisemore after leaving the St Paul's Street terminus. It now carries Walsall number 874 and is on the clockwise Route 30 circular (Walsall-Bloxwich-Blakenall-Walsall). This was the only vehicle not to be lengthened by Walsall. (Author's collection)

(left)   118. As indicated earlier three of the BUTs were rebuilt by Walsall being lengthened and fitted with front entrances. One of the trio, Cleethorpes 62 (later 162) and now numbered 877 in the Walsall fleet, is seen leaving St Paul's bus station on Route 15 to Blakenall in June 1963. The upper deck window inserts can be clearly seen whilst on the lower deck the five window bays have been moved rearwards. (M Dryhurst)

(lower left)   119. The tower blocks in the background of this view give the photograph an Eastern European feel as Cleethorpes Crossley 63 (later 163) is seen as 850 in the all over blue livery of Walsall Corporation. It is on the anti-clockwise circular Route 15 (Walsall-Blakenall-Bloxwich-Walsall) and is passing through Blakenall Heath en route to Bloxwich. The vehicle seems to be high on its springs especially at the front end in this May 1963 view. (D F Parker)

120. This view shows what is probably the most unusual initiative of Mr Edgley-Cox when he was the Walsall General Manager. Cleethorpes Crossley 64 (later 164), now Walsall 873, has had the lower deck rear end cut away to allow for the experimental mounting of a diesel engine which can be seen fitted to the guarded cantilevered platform. Presumably the idea was to create a hybrid vehicle that could be used in either form of propulsion; it is reported that the vehicle ran along the unopened M6 on trade plates in diesel format. (A Colley)

MP Middleton Press

Easebourne Lane, Midhurst, West Sussex. GU29 9AZ Tel:01730 813169

EVOLVING THE ULTIMATE RAIL ENCYCLOPEDIA

www.middletonpress.co.uk email:info@middletonpress.co.uk

A-0 906520 B-1 873793 C-1 901706 D-1 904474

OOP Out of Print at time of printing - Please check current availability **BROCHURE AVAILABLE SHOWING NEW TITLES**

A
Abergavenny to Merthyr C 91 5
Abertillery and Ebbw Vale Lines D 84 5
Aldgate & Stepney Tramways B 70 7
Allhallows - Branch Line to A 62 2
Alton - Branch Lines to A 11 8
Andover to Southampton A 82 7
Ascot - Branch Lines around A 64 9
Ashburton - Branch Line to B 95 2
Ashford - Steam to Eurostar B 67 7
Ashford to Dover A 48 7
Austrian Narrow Gauge D 04 7
Avonmouth - BL around D 42 X
B
Banbury to Birmingham D 27 6
Barking to Southend C 80 X
Barnet & Finchley Tramways B 93 6
Barry - Branch Lines around D 50 0
Basingstoke to Salisbury A 89 4
Bath Green Park to Bristol C 36 2
Bath to Evercreech Junction A 60 6
Bath Tramways B 86 3
Battle over Portsmouth 1940 A 29 0
Battle over Sussex 1940 A 79 7
Bedford to Wellingborough D 31 4
Betwixt Petersfield & Midhurst A 94 0
Blitz over Sussex 1941-42 B 35 9
Bodmin - Branch Lines around B 83 9
Bognor at War 1939-45 B 59 6
Bombers over Sussex 1943-45 B 51 0
Bournemouth & Poole Trys B 47 2
Bournemouth to Evercreech Jn A 46 0
Bournemouth to Weymouth A 57 6
Bournemouth Trolleybuses C 10 9
Bradford Trolleybuses D 19 5
Brecon to Neath D 43 8
Brecon to Newport D 16 0
Brickmaking in Sussex B 19 7
Brightons Tramways B 02 2 OOP
Brighton to Eastbourne A 16 9
Brighton to Worthing A 03 7
Brighton Trolleybuses D 34 9
Bristols Tramways B 57 X
Bristol to Taunton D 03 9
Bromley South to Rochester B 23 5
Bromsgrove to Gloucester D 73 X
Brunel - A railtour of his achievements D 74 8
Bude - Branch Line to B 29 4
Burnham to Evercreech Jn A 68 1
Burton & Ashby Tramways C 51 6
C
Camberwell & West Norwood Tys B 22 7
Cambridge to Ely D 55 1
Canterbury - Branch Lines around B 58 8
Cardiff Trolleybuses D 64 0
Caterham & Tattenham Corner B 25 1
Changing Midhurst C 15 X
Chard and Yeovil - BLs around C 30 3
Charing Cross to Dartford A 75 4
Charing Cross to Orpington A 96 7
Cheddar - Branch Line to B 90 1
Cheltenham to Andover C 43 5
Cheltenham to Redditch D 81 0
Chesterfield Tramways D 37 3
Chesterfield Trolleybuses D 51 9
Chichester to Portsmouth A 14 2
Clapham & Streatham Trys B 97 9 OOP
Clapham Junction - 50 yrs C 06 0 OOP
Clapham Junction to Beckenham Jn B 36 7
Clevedon & Portishead - BLs to D 18 7
Collectors Trains, Trolleys & Trams D 29 2
Colonel Stephens D62 4
Cornwall Narrow Gauge D 56 X
Crawley to Littlehampton A 34 7
Cromer - Branch Lines around C 26 5
Croydons Tramways B 42 1
Croydons Trolleybuses B 73 1 OOP
Croydon to East Grinstead B 48 0
Crystal Palace (HL) & Catford Loop A 87 8
D
Darlington Trolleybuses D 33 0
Dartford to Sittingbourne B 34 0
Derby Tramways D 17 9
Derby Trolleybuses C 72 9
Derwent Valley - Branch Line to the D 06 3
Didcot to Banbury D 02 0
Didcot to Swindon C 84 2
Didcot to Winchester C 13 3
Dorset & Somerset Narrow Gauge D 76 4
Douglas to Peel C 88 5
Douglas to Port Erin C 55 9
Douglas to Ramsey D 39 X
Dovers Tramways B 24 3
Dover to Ramsgate A 78 9

E
Ealing to Slough C 42 7
Eastbourne to Hastings A 27 4 OOP
East Cornwall Mineral Railways D 22 5
East Croydon to Three Bridges A 53 3
East Grinstead - Branch Lines to A 07 X
East Ham & West Ham Tramways B 52 9
East Kent Light Railway A 61 4 OOP
East London - Branch Lines of C 44 3
East London Line B 80 4
East Ridings Secret Resistance D 21 7
Edgware & Willesden Tramways C 18 4
Effingham Junction - BLs around A 74 6
Eltham & Woolwich Tramways B 74 X OOP
Ely to Kings Lynn C 53 2
Ely to Norwich C 90 7
Embankment & Waterloo Tramways B 41 3
Enfield & Wood Green Trys C 03 6 OOP
Enfield Town & Palace Gates - BL to D 32 2
Epsom to Horsham A 30 4
Euston to Harrow & Wealdstone C 89 3
Exeter & Taunton Tramways B 32 4
Exeter to Barnstaple B 15 4
Exeter to Newton Abbot C 49 4
Exeter to Tavistock B 69 3
Exmouth - Branch Lines to B 00 6
F
Fairford - Branch Line to A 52 5
Falmouth, Helston & St. Ives - BL to C 74 5
Fareham to Salisbury A 67 3
Faversham to Dover B 05 7
Felixstowe & Aldeburgh - BL to D 20 9
Fenchurch Street to Barking C 20 6
Festiniog - 50 yrs of enterprise C 83 4
Festiniog in the Fifties B 68 5
Festiniog in the Sixties B 91 X
Finsbury Park to Alexandra Palace C 02 8
Frome to Bristol B 77 4
Fulwell - Trams, Trolleys & Buses D 11 X
G
Gloucester to Bristol D 35 7
Gloucester to Cardiff D 66 7
Gosport & Horndean Trys B 92 8
Gosport - Branch Lines around A 36 3
Great Yarmouth Tramways D 13 6
Greece Narrow Gauge D 72 1
Greenwich & Dartford Tramways B 14 6 OOP
Grimsby & Cleethorpes Trolleybuses D 86 1
Guildford to Redhill A 63 0 OOP
H
Hammersmith & Hounslow Trys C 33 8
Hampshire Narrow Gauge D 36 5
Hampshire Waterways A 84 3 OOP
Hampstead & Highgate Tramways B 53 7
Harrow to Watford D 14 4
Hastings to Ashford A 37 1
Hastings Tramways B 18 9
Hastings Trolleybuses B 81 2 OOP
Hawkhurst - Branch Line to A 66 5
Hayling - Branch Line to A 12 6
Haywards Heath to Seaford A 28 2
Henley, Windsor & Marlow - BL to C77 X
Hereford to Newport D 54 3
Hexham to CarlisleD 75 6
Hitchin to Peterborough D 07 1
Holborn & Finsbury Tramways B 79 0
Holborn Viaduct to Lewisham A 81 9
Horsham - Branch Lines to A 02 9
Huddersfield Trolleybuses C 92 3
Hull Tramways D60 8
Hull Trolleybuses D 24 1
Huntingdon - Branch Lines around A 93 2
I
Ilford & Barking Tramways B 61 8
Ilford to Shenfield C 97 4
Ilfracombe - Branch Line to B 21 9
Ilkeston & Glossop Tramways D 40 3
Industrial Rlys of the South East A 09 6
Ipswich to Saxmundham C 41 9
Ipswich Trolleybuses D 59 4
Isle of Wight Lines - 50 yrs C 12 5
K
Keighley Tramways & Trolleybuses D 83 7
Kent & East Sussex Waterways A 72 X
Kent Narrow Gauge C 45 1
Kent Seaways - Hoys to Hovercraft D 79 9
Kingsbridge - Branch Line to C 98 2
Kingston & Hounslow Loops A 83 5 OOP
Kingston & Wimbledon Tramways B 56 1
Kingswear - Branch Line to C 17 6
L
Lambourn - Branch Line to C 70 2
Launceston & Princetown - BL to C 19 2
Lewisham & Catford Tramways B 26 X OOP

Lewisham to Dartford A 92 4
Lines around Wimbledon B 75 8
Liverpool Street to Chingford D 01 2
Liverpool Street to Ilford C 34 6
Liverpool Tramways - Eastern C 04 4
Liverpool Tramways - Northern C 46 X
Liverpool Tramways - Southern C 23 0
London Bridge to Addiscombe B 20 0
London Bridge to East Croydon A 58 4
London Chatham & Dover Railway A 88 6
London Termini - Past and Proposed D 00 4
London to Portsmouth Waterways B 43 X
Longmoor - Branch Lines to A 41 X
Looe - Branch Line to C 22 2
Lyme Regis - Branch Line to A 45 2
Lynton - Branch Line to B 04 9
M
Maidstone & Chatham Tramways B 40 5
Maidstone Trolleybuses C 00 1 OOP
March - Branch Lines around B 09 X
Margate & Ramsgate Tramways C 52 4
Marylebone to Rickmansworth D49 7
Midhurst - Branch Lines around A 49 5
Midhurst - Branch Lines to A 01 0 OOP
Military Defence of West Sussex A 23 1
Military Signals, South Coast C 54 0
Minehead - Branch Line to A 80 0
Mitcham Junction Lines B 01 4
Mitchell & company C 59 1
Monmouthshire Eastern Valleys D 71 3
Moreton-in-Marsh to Worcester D 26 8
Moretonhampstead - BL to C 27 3
Mountain Ash to Neath D 80 2
N
Newbury to Westbury C 66 4
Newcastle to Hexham D 69 1
Newcastle Trolleybuses D 78 0
Newport (IOW) - Branch Lines to A 26 6
Newquay - Branch Lines to C 71 0
Newton Abbot to Plymouth C 60 5
Northern France Narrow Gauge C 75 3
North East German Narrow Gauge D 44 6
North Kent Tramways B 44 8
North London Line B 94 4
North Woolwich - BLs around C 65 6
Norwich Tramways C 40 0
Nottinghamshire & Derbyshire T/B D 63 2
Nottinghamshire & Derbyshire T/W D 53 5
O
Orpington to Tonbridge B 03 0 OOP
Oxford to Bletchley D57 8
Oxford to Moreton-in-Marsh D 15 2
P
Paddington to Ealing C 37 0
Paddington to Princes Risborough C 81 8
Padstow - Branch Line to B 54 5
Plymouth - BLs around B 98 7
Plymouth to St. Austell C 63 X
Pontypool to Mountain Ash D 65 9
Porthmadog 1954-94 - BL around B 31 6
Porthmadog to Blaenau B 50 2 OOP
Portmadoc 1923-46 - BL around B 13 8
Portsmouths Tramways B 72 3
Portsmouth to Southampton A 31 2
Portsmouth Trolleybuses C 73 7
Potters Bar to Cambridge D 70 5
Princes Risborough - Branch Lines to D 05 5
Princes Risborough to Banbury C 85 0
R
Railways to Victory C 16 8/7 OOP
Reading to Basingstoke B 27 8
Reading to Didcot C 79 6
Reading to Guildford A 47 9 OOP
Reading Tramways B 87 1
Reading Trolleybuses C 05 2
Redhill to Ashford A 73 8
Return to Blaenau 1970-82 C 64 8
Rickmansworth to Aylesbury D 61 6
Roman Roads of Hampshire D 67 5
Roman Roads of Surrey C 61 3
Roman Roads of Sussex C 48 6
Romneyrail C 32 X
Ryde to Ventnor A 19 3
S
Salisbury to Westbury B 39 1
Salisbury to Yeovil B 06 5 OOP
Saxmundham to Yarmouth C 69 9
Saxony Narrow Gauge D 47 0
Seaton & Eastbourne Tramways B 76 6 OOP
Seaton & Sidmouth - Branch Lines to A 95 9
Secret Sussex Resistance B 82 0
SECR Centenary album C 11 7
Selsey - Branch Line to B 04 9
Sheerness - Branch Lines around B 16 2

Shepherds Bush to Uxbridge T/W
Shrewsbury - Branch Line to A 86
Sierra Leone Narrow Gauge D 28
Sittingbourne to Ramsgate A 90 8
Slough to Newbury C 56 7
Solent - Creeks, Crafts & Cargoes
Southamptons Tramways B 33 2
Southampton to Bournemouth A 4
Southend-on-Sea Tramways B 28
Southern France Narrow Gauge C
Southwark & Deptford Tramways
Southwold - Branch Line to A 15 0
South Eastern & Chatham Railwa
South London Line B 46 4
South London Tramways 1903-33
St. Albans to Bedford D 08 X
St. Austell to Penzance C 67 2
St. Pancras to Barking D 68 3
St. Pancras to St. Albans C 78 8
Stamford Hill Tramways B 85 5
Steaming through Cornwall B 30 8
Steaming through Kent A 13 4 OO
Steaming through the Isle of Wight
Steaming through West Hants A 69
Stratford upon avon to Birmingha
Stratford upon Avon to Cheltenham
Strood to Paddock Wood B 12 X O
Surrey Home Guard C 57 5
Surrey Narrow Gauge C 87 7
Surrey Waterways A 51 7 OOP
Sussex Home Guard C 24 9
Sussex Narrow Gauge C 68 0
Sussex Shipping Sail, Steam & Mot
Swanley to Ashford B 45 6
Swindon to Bristol C 96 6
Swindon to Gloucester D46 2
Swindon to Newport D 30 6
Swiss Narrow Gauge C 94 X
T
Talyllyn - 50 years C 39 7
Taunton to Barnstaple B 60 X
Taunton to Exeter C 82 6
Tavistock to Plymouth B 88 X
Tees-side Trolleybuses D 58 6
Tenterden - Branch Line to A 21 5
Thanet's Tramways B 11 1 OOP
Three Bridges to Brighton A 35 5
Tilbury Loop C 86 9
Tiverton - Branch Lines around C 6
Tivetshall to Beccles D 41 1
Tonbridge to Hastings A 44 4
Torrington - Branch Lines to B 37 5
Tunbridge Wells - Branch Lines to A
Twickenham & Kingston Trys C 35
Two-Foot Gauge Survivors C 21 4 O
U
Upwell - Branch Line to B 64 2
V
Victoria & Lambeth Tramways B 49
Victoria to Bromley South A 98 3
Victoria to East Croydon A 40 1 OOP
Vivarais C 31 1 OOP
W
Walthamstow & Leyton Tramways
Waltham Cross & Edmonton Trys C
Wandsworth & Battersea Tramways
Wantage - Branch Line to D 25 X
Wareham to Swanage - 50 yrs D 09 8
War on the Line A 10 X
War on the Line VIDEO + 88 0
Waterloo to Windsor A 54 1
Waterloo to Woking A 38 X
Watford to Leighton Buzzard D 45 4
Wenford Bridge to Fowey C 09 5
Westbury to Bath B 55 3
Westbury to Taunton C 76 1
West Cornwall Mineral Railways D 4
West Croydon to Epsom B 08 1
West London - Branch Lines of C 50 8
West London Line B 84 7
West Sussex Waterways A 24 X OOP
West Wiltshire - Branch Lines of D 12
Weymouth - Branch Lines around A
Willesden Junction to Richmond B 71
Wimbledon to Beckenham C 58 3
Wimbledon to Epsom B 62 6
Wimborne - Branch Lines around A 9
Wisbech - Branch Lines around C 01
Wisbech 1800-1901 C 93 1
Woking to Alton A 59 2
Woking to Portsmouth A 25 8
Woking to Southampton A 55 X
Wolverhampton Trolleybuses D 77 X
Woolwich & Dartford Trolleys B 66 9
Worcester to Hereford D 38 X
Worthing to Chichester A 06 1
Y
Yeovil - 50 yrs change C 38 9
Yeovil to Dorchester A 76 2 OOP
Yeovil to Exeter A 91 6
York Tramways & Trolleybuses D 82 9